THE 90 DAY AUTHOR

THE 90 DAY AUTHOR

VALERIE SHERROD

Sherrodpublishing

LARGO, MD

The 90 Day Author

ISBN-13: 978-0-9707750-9-2 (*sc*)
LCCN: 2013902372

Printed in the United States of America.

Published by:

The 90 Day Author
An imprint of Sherrod Publishing and Enterprises

www.the90dayauthor.com
www.sherrodpublishing.com
valerie@the90dayauthor.com

Dedication

This book is dedicated to Vicki Irvin. Thank you for bringing The 90 Day Author to life. You are an empowering woman who has challenged me to bring Business, Beauty and Balance into my life.

A special dedication to Teresa Neely.
You are an IT geek but also a friend and voice of reason. Thank you for your wisdom and being on my side. Your calm nature has affected me in a very special way.

To James Sherrod, my beloved brother whom I can talk to about anything in this world.

I especially dedicate this book to business owners and aspiring business owners. In your field of expertise lies a gem. The gem is a book inside of you that's waiting to be read by others.

Acknowledgements

I feel blessed and honored by the God of the Universe to be alive, to feel His presence each morning, and to be a part of His divine plan for my life. I believe in the principle:

"To whom much is given, much is required"

An overwhelming gratitude to my Mastermind group, the movers and shakers—Anene, Becky, Karen, Marie, Markita, Mary, Missy, Sophia, Vicki, and Yolanda. Your steadfastness, inspiration, valuable input, and energy propel me to move forward. It is amazing to be among women who are able to strategize, put a plan in place and take fast action.

Contents

Contents

Planting Your Flag on the Moon

*W*hat if you were given the chance to define not only your company, but also your entire profession or industry? You could set pricing, establish standards, censor the competition and in general become the person who makes the rules the others must follow. Interested?

What if this could be accomplished in just 90 days? Still reading? Good. Then go and write the book.

That's not a flippant one-liner. It's a statement of fact.

Our world is full of frontiers and undefined boundaries. A geographer from Wales was responsible for surveying a major portion of India and they named a mountain after him. It wasn't just any mountain, but the tallest in the world. He traversed unmapped areas of the world and his work defined boundaries, and established dominions. Ironically, he was just doing his job.

Your business may not be surveying mountaintops but you have the potential of being as respected in your own profession.

We are currently at a time in history that may never come again. There has been a fundamental shift in the power of persuasion. All that's left is for you to figure out where you fit in.

There has been a fundamental shift in the power of persuasion.

The Internet has been a great equalizer. Joe Blow's Car Manufacturing on the corner can control as much Internet real estate as any major car manufacturer. It's not a matter of budget since Internet real estate is practically free. If Joe Blow is willing to put up the relevant content, he will even rank higher in search engine results. The only thing remaining to be seen is whether Joe Blow is savvy enough to recognize the opportunity that lies before him.

Network television is being systematically replaced by cable channels whose sophisticated, well-written series are now cleaning up at the Emmys. Radio no longer has a dial, but a URL. Newspaper notables are now scrambling for blog space with Internet newbies. Even major news companies are encouraging its viewers to follow them on social media for even more current updates. Do you realize that as of this writing, social media is approximately nine-years old?

eBooks were introduced at the 2005 Book Expo—the largest bookselling show in the world. Curious writers marveled at the ingenuity but the publishers attending commented with disdain, "Very pretty, but no one will ever read a book on a computer. You can't take that into the bathtub or to the beach." In 2012, approximately 200 million iPads were sold—just one of the eReader offerings on the market. Well, evidently, *someone* is reading on the computer and *yes,* they do make an app for that.

Major software companies are opening in China. One out of every five people on the planet lives in China. Does anyone want to guess how many iPads that adds up to? It is forecasted that in 2013, half the books sold on the planet will be eBooks.

If your readers are in the group who are still clinging to their paper, the majority of copies they hold were printed digitally. This means one-at-a-time. No inventory. No waste. 24-hour delivery. Updated at a key-click.

What this shift has done is to put the power of definition into the hands of the people who live it, work in it, and train for it. There are more words written on foreign policy by young people texting while witnessing it than all the ambassadors' statements in the world. History is being chronicled by search engines, which have a limitless memory, and loves to cache.

How do you get a piece of it?

It all starts with just…one…book.

Chapter 1

Move Over Traditional Publishers

*T*raditional publishers may be looking for the exit, but book publishing is not. Just less than a decade ago an author had the daunting task of finding an agent to represent them. It wasn't permissible to contact a publisher directly. Some say agents were even harder to land. Your odds of getting a contract as a new author were less than 1%. This discouraged a great many authors and certainly limited the amount of knowledge that the public could access.

The electronic age has changed all that. The customers are still there; their method of getting their reading material is all that has changed. That, however, is not all that makes this period in history unique.

With the shift in *how* information is dispersed comes the responsibility of generating or authoring that information. By the economical suicide of traditional publishing, those big name companies have also lost the power of influence. In short, the old boys' network is no longer calling the shots.

Independent authors are now clustered in the top positions at amazon.com. While the traditionalists call *foul*, citing poor quality by Indy writers. Ask yourself the last time you wandered into a bookstore and asked to see only the books published by the big houses. The truth is, it doesn't matter who publishes a book; it only matters whether people buy it.

So…here we are. A period in time where reading is not only convenient, affordable and actually fashionable—but the opportunity to become an author is wide open. Perhaps more importantly, content in the form of a book, paper or electronic, is still more highly respected than random statements on a website. People still associate books with the integrity earned by notable people. Even our legal system encourages clients to operate by placing everything in writing.

When we say the opportunity is wide open, that's an understatement. Absolutely anyone can publish a book. Somehow, unfortunately, business has been the last kid in the classroom door.

For some reason, business has been one of the last entities to recognize this opportunity. Perhaps it is because they are so consumed with the everyday survival mode of running a business that now has global competition. Then again, it may be because everyone is afraid to step forward to claim the flag, hoping to follow in a well-trod footstep rather than commit to the time and authority it takes to publish a book.

A real book.

This is no time for corporate cowardice. Your opportunity will pass as technology rockets forward into the future. Right now is that very unique period when credible business information is *People value books. You have the information. They want your books. It's simple.* first being fed to the public at large. People value books. You have the information. They want your books. It's simple.

It's More Than Numbers

In the age of the Internet and network television that caters to the lowest common denominator, marketing is all about the eye time. How many commercials can you pack into the commercial breakaway of a Super Bowl game? Can you really distinguish between the content of a reality TV episode and the beauty products commercials laced therein?

How much advertise placements can a company throw at you before the screen becomes a nuisance and you switch to overload? How much time have you wasted over the past few years ridding yourself of SPAM advertising that filled your Inbox? Can you feel comfortable chatting with Aunt Martha on social media without feeling your privacy invaded by the zip code and keyword-tagged ads that UN-randomly pop up according to your conversation?

It's no secret, the consumption IQ of America has sunk to an all-time low. This contrasts vividly with the opportunity for education. What does that mean for you?

It means that there is an immense void just waiting to be filled. It's called Quality Information. Take the experience and knowledge you have acquired and use it to show the world that you know what you're doing. This is no longer a time where your local competition was all you needed to beat. It's a global economy and if you don't believe that, look at the boarded up buildings in small towns across the U.S. and check out the $1.98 billion dollars spent on Cyber Monday this year alone. That's up over 25% from last year.

Don't you want a piece of that? How do you get it? Write the book on your industry. Now! Remember when you could buy almost any domain you could think of? Do you realize there are only a couple of dozen 3-letters domains available on the domain auction block today? Believe me, they're not selling for $8.95. This opportunity comes along every few hundred years.

Okay, Just the Numbers, Please

Still not convinced? Try these on for size.

- Ingram Book Company, the world's largest book distributor has over 30,000 wholesalers
- Ingram's network reaches into 100 countries
- 3.1 billion books were sold in the U.S. last year alone
- Over 200,000 books published last year were from independent authors
- 38% of the books published were non-fiction
- The profit of publishing a book can be whatever you want it to be.
- A traditionally-published author generally receives just 7-11% of the book's list price as royalty, but you can keep 100% in royalty if you self-publish

*Figures courtesy of Publisher's Weekly

Okay, so now let's get this straight. Your company sells widgets. If someone offered you 30,000 instant distributors for your widgets, in 100 countries and you knew that over 3.1 billion widgets sold last year—would you accept their offer? Of course!

I'm Not an Author, I Run a Business

Part of running a successful business is to make mistakes. Mostly, each successful businessperson alive has failed at some point. Ask any multi-billionaire who has filed for bankruptcy. Since we don't all have billionaire-esque assets to play with, it's important to learn from the mistakes others have made.

Everything you know is valuable information for someone. Everything. You may not realize how much you *do* know, actually. Let's say you run a hot dog stand. Let's even say you're successful at it—as hotdog stands go. Now, out there at

> Everything you know is valuable information for someone.

any given time are probably a thousand people contemplating opening a hotdog stand…somewhere. You might even live in a beachside community where someone is considering opening one near your own. "So what do I have to write about?" you ask. There are a couple of different angles here you can pursue. First, there are those thousand or so people who want to open their own business, and would gladly pay ten bucks to learn how to avoid the mistakes you already made. That may only be $10,000 in possible sales, but you have done something else quite miraculous. You've written the first book on how to operate a hotdog stand. Therefore, you are considered an expert.

Now, perhaps this isn't enough for your epitaph so let's take it one-step further. You begin to get emails from some of the folks who bought your book, wondering if you happen to have a franchise opportunity. They liked your book and business model. Thankfully, they would rather buy into your proven ability than do it alone. Now, you have a business opportunity you didn't have before.

So, what else does this do? If forces you to define your business. Now, you must actually look at the bottom line and separate the business sense of what you do from the love of watching the pretty women or handsome men on the nearby beach. You have to analyze which hotdog brand you serve and why it works best for you. You will compare brands of mustard, pickle relish and study the most efficient way to cut up an onion. You will learn to explain how you hire employees and the licensing you need to set up in your community. You might share your advertising strategies; coupons, flyers, ads, whatever. Perhaps you did your homework on branding and ended up with a magnificent sign that attracts customers all on its own. How did you pick the spot where you set up? Is it profitable to stay open all year or how do you know which months to cut out? Do you have a private recipe that draws a crowd? What else do you serve with the dogs? How do you handle flies? Power outages? Thunderstorms? Seating for customers? Is your stand portable or fixed real estate? What would you do differently if you had only known (or read someone else's book)?

It doesn't stop there. Maybe you have a family recipe for pickle relish that your customers rave about. The book establishes you as expert and it's automatically assumed you are a success. Parlay that into finding other outlets for your special hotdog recipe. Maybe the ice cream shop in the next town over wants to sell your hotdogs and you devise a sort of distribution arrangement. They can also sell your book. Make it a creative book, combining not only the story of your business, but the history of the hotdog and 100 different topping suggestions. Now you have something that tourists will love and you can sell the book through gift shops everywhere. Maybe it earns you an invitation to a local cooking show, and then on to a cable network guest spot. Before you know it, your name is a household word and your business is worth a hundred times what it was. You no longer just own a hotdog stand—you are running a hotdog empire. Hotdog manufacturers seek you out for your endorsement; catsup companies want to design a custom package with your logo on it. "As used at Joe's Famous Hotdog Stand."

Worst case? You might learn something about your own business that you didn't already know. What's that worth to you? Now what was that about running a business?

What's in a Book?

*M*aybe your purpose for writing a book isn't as clearly cut as Joe's Hotdog Stand... *yes, that's supposed to be funny.* Seriously, let's look at some other available options.

The Authority Book

A typical profession for this might be an attorney. Perhaps you want to write a guide for people to write their own wills. You can do the research for each of the 50 states and teach people the fundamentals of what is required for a will to be valid in their particular location. You might include some suggestions on how to divide assets when certain circumstances exist— such as a mixed family with children and stepchildren. You might show them how to avoid probate and teach them the related terminology. Explain the concept of power of attorney or owning real estate with rights to survivor.

As you will realize, much of what you discuss will not be available at a self-serve level so show them how to find a competent attorney in their local area. Naturally, this will direct them to you if they're nearby. Besides the obvious boost to your own practice, you have now established yourself as an expert in probate law. Send copies of your book to media and suggest you are available as an expert when needed. One day someone notable will pass into eternity and the press will need an expert to help him or her sort out a probate scandal. Whom are they going to call? Smile, you're on camera!

Even if you publish the book for just yourself, distribute copies to every funeral home in the area and ask them to offer it freely to their families while pre-planning funerals. Offer to include a back-cover ad from that funeral home. This can be a very inexpensive substitution and it completely personalizes the product. When you're done with funeral homes, start with accountants and firms that do tax preparation. These opportunities have only begun. The worst case? You add some clients and meet a number of business people who become good contacts.

This is an example of an authority book. Essentially these are penned by professionals; highly successful or advanced degree individuals who are in a position of...that's right...authority. They are the trendsetters, the people in the know. These are individuals who Joe Blow wants to emulate; they can make anything look simple and within reach.

As we all know, however, just reading a book does not make you an expert. Thus, if you fear that writing a book will create your own competition, that's very unlikely to happen. It's far more likely, that you will contribute to the general awareness of what you do and that may help someone. It may be simply offering a new perspective to a completely unrelated business.

> Just reading a book does not make you an expert.

There's also the very real possibility that you will develop new contacts and opportunities from the exposure.

The most likely return, however, in writing a book about your business or profession is that you stand to gain new customers. There's nothing like a publicity campaign surrounding a book to revive a slumping industry. Consider the examples below:

David's family has operated a small chain of funeral homes for more than three decades. A major corporate competitor recently opened a new location within David's communities. No expense was spared in creating an architecturally modern building with elaborate landscaping, including a walled prayer garden with fountains, marble seating and outdoor sound system. David's facilities were all located in converted private homes and remodeling even one of them would have involved zoning issues and major expense.

David instantly began to see a major drop in his business. Feedback from the community pointed out the slightly haphazard appearance of using one of David's converted homes, while the competitor's location provided an almost celebratory, elegant statement alternative.

David knew the one advantage he had was that his properties were all paid for; they had been acquired gradually throughout the family's long involvement. Thus, his overhead was smaller and therefore he could charge less. Would the community see him as a bargain discounter? He had a serious image problem.

He chose not to defend, but to go on the offensive. David penned a short but detailed guide to planning funerals and little known secrets of his industry that could save families money. Instead of trying to build his own reputation, David concentrated on exposing the disadvantages of using a larger chain company. He stressed assembly-line treatment, the absence of familiar surroundings, and the apathy of being handled by someone who did not know the deceased or the family, and the upselling tactics of a profit-minded company with a major overhead to support. He explained that embalming was not a legal requirement and suggested that families consider renting a larger luxury car and having an extended family member drive rather than pay for the limousine and chauffer the funeral home wanted them to use. This arrangement permitted the immediate family to be picked up from their home, driven not just to the cemetery but also to the luncheon afterwards and then delivered safely home as a group.

His guide was personalized for the communities where he operated and listed valuable information such as how to purchase your own cemetery plot and the fees of the counties involved in opening/closing graves and maintenance. He shared information about available ministers, how to obtain a veteran's flag and included even suggested menus, which could be available from local restaurants in their catering facilities. The book was neutral enough to be practical advice to anyone, but local enough to remind people that they preferred to place their final arrangements with a "friend of the family" rather than a corporate conveyor belt. The fact that David published a book warranted him additional attention by the local newspapers and he was invited to speak at several local organizations about the experience of a business owner turned author.

David's "Goliath-busting" also garnered some attention in his industry as many smaller home operators were facing the same sort of corporate competition. David's book was purchased in bulk by these fellow small community homes, and distributed as a service through estate planning attorneys, churches and florists. The result was that eventually David's book was bringing in more profit than one of his locations. It also guided his decisions in acquiring new properties.

Another strategy for writing your book is to educate your customers. You may own a company that has a limited corporate customer base, but one that could offer options to private individuals if they understood what you have to offer. An example could be security systems. Educate your customers in the many ways they could affordably enhance their lives with modified installations. Perhaps they are caretakers of an elderly family member and a monitoring system with optional mini-cam would allow them to work in the yard or run to the neighbor's and still monitor their loved one's safety. Explain how a properly installed system could pay for itself in lower insurance premiums, vacation housesitting and even, unfortunately, the cost of being a victim of a crime.

Provide the necessary assistance to your customer as they discover the nightmare of a home invasion. Aid them through filling out the police reports, the property insurance forms, the awareness of violation, and through the ongoing trauma of fearing a reoccurrence.

Booksignings? How about sponsoring a women's self-defense clinic and giving a copy of your book away with registration? Host a booth at the local community fair that teaches families how to devise an escape plan in the event of a fire in their home. Anyone requesting a free installation estimate receives a copy of your book.

Think of the number of opportunities you have had over your professional career when you could have benefitted from handing out more than a simple business card.

- Chamber of Commerce dinners
- Church
- Alumni reunions
- Trade Shows
- Professional Days
- Interviews
- Professional functions
- Social gatherings
- Sales calls
- Financial and business negotiations

How about a Creative Book Launch?

You're standing on the dock with a bottle of expensive wine in hand and the ship is awaiting your blessing. That's what it feels like, even if the ship is just your new book. Just?

Does no one appreciate the mindless hours spent researching, checking and crosschecking facts? Does no one understand the efforts to make the topic real and engaging to your readers?

You took the step and now you hold your book in your hands. After all, there are plenty of months ahead for hitting the phones and road to market the book. In this small window of time, let's celebrate!

Everyone likes a party. Almost everyone likes books. So, why do self-publishing authors so often overlook the obvious?

The busy part is now over and it's time to give the book a birthday party. In the publishing industry, lifetimes are short and obscurity beckons. Let's give it a run for the money!

When do we hold it?

Timing can be a very important strategy if you've authored the latest greatest book—yours. More likely, though, the timing is going to be relatively simple. Have the party when the book is broadly available. This doesn't mean when you get your first author's copy, or when you load it on your website. Those should be considered advance copies.

If you've chosen digital publishing, the book will literally live in a computer until each copy is ordered. It will take a commitment from a bookstore to get the first carton shipped and on a shelf.

So, let's get a bookstore to do just that!

Many new authors pester the manager of a local store to order in copies for a first book signing. The signing day comes and the author is seated at their table with a dozen books and a poised pen. They await their first autograph, and await…and await. At the end of the two hours, they pack up their belongings and trudge out the door, trying bravely to keep their shoulders straight and the tear of disappointment from their eye. They just launched their first book, and the world didn't care.

There's a much better way to do this, and to avoid that feeling of rejection. Choosing a signing at the store for your book's launch is only setting yourself up for disappointment. Chances are all those cousins, aunts and uncles who were "so proud" of you, will find something else to do that day and just assume there will be others to cheer you on. Your friends will figure it's a family event and they'll catch you another time. Why? A bookstore is a store and not the place to have a lively party! There is no imagination, no streamers, no microphone and no tables laden with inherited family recipes. It's bo-o-o-o- o-o-ring.

If you're working with the 90 Day Author, leave the party planning to us!

Planning the Party

We're going to get very creative at this point because after all, it is a party. You will want to make a big splash, enough so that people will talk about it and that gets the buzz going.

You must fill that simple human need by introducing your work in such a manner as to make it remarkable, repeatable and in some sense, profitable.

Some authors are too wrapped up in the ego of writing. In addition, some feel the world should beat the proverbial path to their door in adoration. It doesn't work that way. People tend to care about what is only in their own lives and only take part in others' when there is some benefit to do so. You must fill that simple human need by introducing your work in such a manner as to make it remarkable, repeatable and in some sense, profitable.

Therefore, no matter how scholarly your book is, you need to focus on creating excitement. Let's look at some examples.

The Technical Book

Technical books are, by nature, very dry reading. Rarely, are they the book of choice to read on a lazy afternoon. It's generally read to learn a subject clearly and thoroughly, often next to a computer. Let's assume that your book deals with a particular software program.

Set up a computer party. Look for a location where you can get access to several computers in the same room. This might be a computer café, a classroom or maybe you simply host this in a fun location and everyone brings his or her own laptop. This would work best if the software you have written about were available as a trial download. Conduct an impromptu class but play lively music and serve colorful foods. Consider adapting the software's logo colors into your theme; maybe decorate a cake with it, tint the lemonade or champagne (depending on your budget) and don't forget to give your guests a few business cards with your book cover on it so they can pass them around for you.

Speaking of business cards, we should mention here that these wouldn't be set up in the conventional format you might expect. It should be more of a business card for your book, than about you. Include a cover picture, the URL where it may be purchased, the ISBN, price and a very few words which describe it. You could add something helpful on the back, perhaps a small ruler, conversion table, list of holidays, etc. and may even want to laminate the card or add a tassel for a bookmark/business card combination.

Of course, one of the unique locations for a launch party for a technical book would be on the Internet itself. If you don't have chat software on your website, you can get free access to this through many websites. Extend invitations through the social networking sites. Invite everyone you know, and hopefully they know, to be available as you conduct a virtual book launch. This can be coordinated with a live launch party that you stream via a web cam to the visitors in your net-based party.

The Cookbook

You own a restaurant. Naturally, your book is a cookbook! Of course, the most obvious launch party is one where you prepare the recipes you've featured in the book. Afterwards, serve your guests in style. Why not put a spin on this. Instead, break your guest list into groups and assign each one a course meal to prepare themselves, via your recipes? Alternatively, theme the party and serve it al fresco on picnic tables in the backyard. Perhaps your recipes are barbecue. You can bring the picnic tables into the living room, and still cook in the kitchen while it's snowing outdoors. Maybe your recipes are all desserts and you invite all the women in your church to come by Sunday afternoon and bring a fork for a dessert smorgasbord.

Another idea might be to ask your guests to come dressed for a masked ball. At the high point of the evening, select one-half dozen guests and blindfold them. Have them sample your recipes and describe the ingredients as they taste them. Video the taste testing moment and put this on your website as a video podcast. This way, all the visitors to your site will become a part of the launch party and enjoy it vicariously.

The Sports Book

Let's say you've written a book on pro basketball, from the perspective of a fan whose is always stuck in the nosebleed seats. Invite your guests to come dressed like NBA all-stars and set things up in front of your big-screen television with platters of hotdogs, drinks and popcorn nearby. Pre-record the background noise of the crowd gathering before a game for atmosphere purposes. When the "game" begins, turn on the television and play a video you've already prepared with an NBA game "best of" clips, but keep the sound turned off. Armed with a microphone, read from your book and make humorous comments about the game clips, inviting your guests to shout out the things they've always been too shy to call out at the games.

The How-To Book

Let's say you've written a book on quilting. What better launch for a book than to have a one-day quilts show and clinic? Gather up some friends who share your interest and look for a church or community center where you can all display your works and conduct a hands-on clinic.

Interest some quilting machine retailers and fabric shops to assist with demonstrations and provide discount coupons. Ask them to judge the show for the winning quilt. You may want to make a quilt in advance of the show and sell raffle tickets at the door; the money going to a homeless charity. Create a simple quilting project. When guests arrive, give them a needle and a chair and create a community quilt to donate too.

One interesting idea might be to ask all your guests to bring a picture of themselves and to scan these to fabric and create the quilt blocks from that fabric. This can be finished and donated to a local museum; a living testament to the women in the community and the spirit of cooperation.

Why is this last idea particularly helpful? It is an idea that will land you media attention. Contact the local newspaper and human interest reporter from the television networks and ask them to send over a camera crew. In addition, film it yourself and send the film directly to media outlets. With any success, you'll see some airtime. If your crowd is especially large, think of the possibility of being picked up by a network. All this—and your book stands the publicity!

Chapter

3

Identifying Your Ideal Reader

When the book was being written, did you keep your reader in mind as a consumer of whatever you wrote, or did you write to feed that audience? It is important to distinguish between the two because it greatly affects how you market your book.

For example, if you wanted your reader to like whatever you wrote, regardless of who they were, you will have a much harder time finding your audience. That's because you have defined them by the nature and topic of your book. Thus, when you go out to begin marketing, you will need to use the search terms that describe your book only and see who you find by spreading your information via that route. You will look for Internet sites, organizations, companies and retailers whose products match the type of book you have written. This is a bit more complicated as you have to maintain external perspective about your book and totally remove your ego from the picture.

For example, if you have written a book about golf, you will not be looking for a specific segment of the population who plays golf; you will be looking for a business entity that caters to players of the game of golf. Your audience will include females, males, children, all ages and all other basic criteria to define a popular segment.

Thus, your search may take you to golf courses, restaurants in golf courses, books that are displayed in golf pro shops, sporting goods stores which sell golfing paraphernalia, golf magazines, golf clubhouses and private courses, etc. Your marketing will be quite broad so that everyone and everything in the game of golf is included.

Now let's put that on the other hand. Let's say you wrote a book about golf but that it's aimed at retired, senior golfers. This puts an entirely different slant on your potential marketing. Not only do you have the golf perspective, but also you can include anyone over the age of 55. This includes members of retirement organizations, retired executives, people of upper income level, professionals, people living in warm climates and people who live in colder climates but are getting ready to retire and move south. Since everyone is going to retire at some point, you have terrifically increased your audience.

Now, instead of simply talking about the game of golf— you are now talking about the future and keeping fit, the game of golf as a pastime and retirement communities where golfing is the game to beat. You're including clothing lines, retirement communities, apartments, condos, other "older people" cars, vitamins and pharmaceuticals, the healthcare industry, senior sports, travel, financial advisors, banks, beauty shops, and anything having to do with grandchildren and family gatherings. Do you see all the connections you've built into the book?

That's why writing for an audience is such an important point to consider when the writing process is still ongoing.

So, who exactly is your ideal reader? Below are some of the criteria you will want to consider:

➢ Sex
➢ Marital status
➢ Education
➢ Age group
➢ Religion or spiritual beliefs
➢ Race or ethnic origin
➢ Income
➢ Organization or club affiliation
➢ Hobbies
➢ Common interests or unifying factor
➢ Accessibility
➢ Shopping habits
➢ Intelligence
➢ Entertainment sources
➢ Profession
➢ Goals
➢ Health
➢ Family
➢ Location
➢ Political affiliation
➢ Undefined or lack of any of the foregoing

"Lack of the foregoing" simply means that your reader falls outside the foregoing criteria. This defines them just as clearly as if they were within a specific group.

Don't confuse identifying criteria with profiling; these are entirely different things. You may think you understand the reading, shopping, worshipping, entertainment habits of a specific group, but a little quality research can show you that you are very mistaken. We tend to assume these qualifying factors based on the people we personally know who fall into these groups.

There is considerable information out there on determining marketing preferences and it's definitely worthwhile to read while you are still writing your book. To supplement that, while you are still writing, try interviewing people you feel may become ideal readers. Ask them what they look for when they read, whether they are looking for specific information or general edification. Ask whether they buy a book because of its cover, because their friends recommend it or whether they simply go by gut instinct when browsing in a bookstore.

Ask what current topics they find important in their lives and their opinion on these topics. Learn where they like to shop and how much they are willing to spend for a book of your genre. This is all valuable marketing information that can help you include the right hooks you'll need to connect to your readers.

Another way to research the demographics is to refer to topical publications or television shows. Spend some time in senior citizen communities and see what kind of billboards are in the area, what radio stations they listen to and the newspapers they are reading. Many seniors are strictly income-based. You'll want to understand that they will, for the most part, probably be borrowing your book from the library rather than making an outright purchase. How can you still profit from that sort of distribution? What sort of advertisers can you interest to reach that market? The purpose of your book may entirely change.

Where does your reader live? They may be in larger metropolitan areas or the small towns of Middle America. Their buying habits will change from region to region as customs and societal backgrounds shape their purchases. Again, there are many sources of demographics available and a good place to check out is your public library.

BECOME A

LEADING AUTHORITY

IN YOUR FIELD OF EXPERTISE

Moving Your Book to Audio/Video

Books and writing isn't just about paper any longer. The electronic revolution has come to publishing.

The Internet has become the new media and brought with it an entirely new palette of creative tools. Authors whose complimenting talents allow them to create art, music, video, interactive learning, photography or puzzles are now in a position to use those skills and take their books well beyond their confines of the printed sheet. There is literally an explosion of imagination and learning options within reach.

We will explore some of these options in this piece and the basics of how to accomplish them. The very nature of creativity, however, will suggest new techniques for you so don't be afraid to explore.

eBooks

Be prepared to read more about eBooks. While they have actually been around since the '90s, it has taken almost a decade for people to warm up to the idea of reading on computers or reading devices. Becoming accustomed to electronic reading is an adjustment. Within the two younger generations, the inundation of computers may have contributed to a reader's preference for the printed copy. Nevertheless, the trend toward e-reading is the hottest movement in the market.

This is spurred by the economic situation in publishing. Who makes the money in the publishing industry? The delivery company, the postal service or a trucking firm are the ones making money. Why? Moving paper is heavy and therefore, expensive. Consider the manufacturing process:

- ➢ trees are sawed and hauled to the ground
- ➢ the paper is then shipped to warehouses awaiting purchase
- ➢ from the warehouse, the paper is sent to the printer and then to a distribution warehouse in the form of books to await purchase
- ➢ the next trip is to the bookseller or directly to the author, who will haul them around from signings to events
- ➢ finally, they reach the hands of the consumer

What that means is each book is shipped in some sense at least five times before reaching the consumer's hands.

Electronic books, however, literally never touch a single hand. They do not require packaging, shelving, moving, and inventories. Yet, they contain the same essence of the author's creation, as does the paper book. They can still be shared, stored and kept indefinitely. Publishers need not deal with book returns that are dirty and unsalable and the landfills are not loaded with cast off paper. Electronic reading is an economic certainty.

Types of eBooks

eBooks come in different flavors.

The one you will hear the most about is that which requires an electronic reading device. These devices have mutated as e-reading developed. Some of the earlier readers were perfectly good devices, but the public simply wasn't ready and they failed. The public acceptance was hindered by two powerful notions.

The publishing industry is very old and practices time-honored business models. For the most part, computers did not even find their way into a publishing office until after the new millennium. That's rather curious when you consider that the computer keyboard is probably the most natural tool a writer/publisher would use. For a traditional publishing model to endure, it must discredit anything that challenges it. When digital printing and electronic reading became possible challengers, the traditional publishing world fought back by diminishing the talent of the writers themselves. The circulated concept was, unless a book publisher of some stature purchased the rights to a work and released it through bookstores, that author couldn't be taken seriously. That is the equivalent of saying that every man who can accurately throw a baseball with speed and consistency is only playing major league baseball. In truth, the traditional publishers chose to cap the number of new authors whose works entered the market and therefore keep the demand from the public high. As digital publishing suddenly allowed a low-cost entry into stores, traditional publishing could only scream about quality, not realizing that the buying public would determine which cream rose to the top; the publishers were not needed.

The reading devices were not well marketed and were perceived as expensive toys with limited few quality books available. The alternative was reading on a desktop computer, as laptops had not yet attained the portability and battery life they have today. Many people still nurtured the "read in the bathtub" visage and computers certainly did not fit in.

This has all changed. The core of the traditional publishing base has been eroded by just exactly what they feared most; new publishers and an onslaught of new and, yes, talented authors. The electronic readers are advancing to market today in rapid succession and their capabilities allow people to read pretty much anywhere they please (bathtub still excepted, but whoever treated a beautiful hardcover book to a bath?)

Amazon made huge headlines in 2007 with the announcement of their Kindle reader. Book club gurus took stock (literally or figuratively) and encouraged their audience to buy their book club suggestions in the Kindle format. That kind of public announcement is hard to overlook and the rage toward e-reading finally found a foothold.

Multimedia Books

Although eBooks are hot, the latest and unequalled version of those is multimedia books, or mBooks. These are essentially multimedia-enhanced eBooks and offer the author the additional tools of sound, color, video, interactivity and a direct connection to the Internet. The implication of this tool is mammoth and really more than we can deal with here. However, marketing your book should definitely include having an eBook, and preferably an mBook format.

So now what?

What does this mean to an author? It means that suddenly you have millions of bookstores to sell through. Literally, any website can sell an eBook and the readers can find niches of topics that are custom tailored to what they want to read. There has literally never been a better time for an author.

How does this help you market your paper book? We will list a few ways:

Make sure you have your paper book available in a number of eBook formats. The most common is .pdf, followed closely by the .epub and the .mobi. Either or both these formats will get keep you compatible with almost every e-reading device on the market today. By offering your book through these readers, you have increased your bookstore availability. This feeds the consumer's desire for instant gratification. They can download the book in under a minute and begin reading immediately. Talk about capitalizing on impulse sales!

Distribute your book's preview in electronic format. This is a very inexpensive way to give readers a taste of the nature of your book. This also gives you an audience with people who like to read paper and those who prefer to read on their electronic reading device, whether that is their desktop, laptop, e-reader or cell phone. Be sure to include a link where your paper book may be purchased. It's always a good idea to add a bit of extra content that may not be found in the book—this is an incentive to download the preview. One concept of that is to advertise bonus content on the cover of your book. This will alert customers they are receiving more for the price of their purchase. Include the content in the eBook (preferably in .pdf and ideally in multimedia eBook format) and make it available from your website. This can take the form of color graphics, photos, audio, screensavers, calendars, tool tips, how-to videos, etc.

Create an eBook trailer, similar to a movie trailer but one that is based on the book and particularly the cover. It creates an attractive and enticing preview introduction to the book and can be a creation unto itself. Put this on your website as a Flash video and let visitors preview your book coming attraction! Invite other related websites to offer a preview eBook from their site. Webmasters are always looking for solid, pertinent, fresh content. By supplying that for them in the nature of both a brief article on your topic, accompanied by a small informational eBook, you're sure to be featured and probably invited back. You're helping to build others site traffic and yours at the same time; don't forget to include a link to your website.

Getting a sponsor for your eBook allows them to advertise in a colorful, inexpensive means to a targeted audience. Consider the ad for hair care products featured in your book about hair. eBooks are a great way to accomplish this.

Write an eBook on a topic that relates to your primary book and offer it for other webmasters to add to their sites. Be sure to include a link to your site, and book purchasing information in the footer of each page. This builds your reputation as an expert, lets you take advantage of other sites' customers and draw traffic to your own site, consequently building your search engine position. These are all very positive networking techniques.

How Do I Sell an eBook?

The key here is distribution. Let's examine some ways you can obtain this.

Your website. It's simple to get a merchant account on your website, but be sure the account permits digital downloads. This means you can capture credit card information via through your account and the funds are distributed straight to your checking account. A digital fulfillment handles the details and after the purchase is made, sends a link where the book may be downloaded, or delivers the book itself. Be sure to include a link to your site in your email signature. Also, include a link in your blog posts and the pertinent, popular blogs you encounter throughout the Internet. Think of it as leaving breadcrumbs that all lead back to your website. This is probably the simplest way to distribute your book.

Affiliates. This means you get others to sell your book on their websites in return for a percentage of commission. Many shopping carts offer affiliate options and this generates a string of code, which the affiliate will embed in their web page. When someone clicks on a link at that site, it brings them to your site but the link includes a string of code which your shopping cart tracks and attributes to your affiliate. You simply establish a percentage of commission in your offering. In addition, be sure to pay in regularly and promptly. This works particularly well if your topic is popular and has many sites connected to it. You can also set up multiple websites yourself and have them link back to you, although be sure to have pertinent, original copy on each one as duplicating copy can get you barred from the search engines and that's not going to help you in the least.

eBook sellers. There are a growing number of eBook bookstores on the Web. Some are regular bookstores that include an eBook section. This can be a dedicated site or a seller like iTunes, Amazon or Barnes & Noble who hosts an eBook area. In the case of Barnes & Noble, they also sell two dedicated eBook readers, so this is particularly an attractive option. Most sites will have a section (often mentioned as a footnote) for publishers/authors. Look for this information and it will guide you through the steps needed to establish a relationship with them. Be prepared that they will likely keep a healthy portion of the sale, but since there is no paper cost involved here, it is often worth it. In essence, you are purchasing the right to present your product to their established customer base. Building a customer base is a time-consuming, expensive undertaking and that is their value. Some authors are resentful about the large percentage booksellers will keep, but when you consider what it cost them to gain their customers and maintain their bookselling infrastructure, it makes far better sense to work with them than to try to duplicate their efforts on your own. The percentage they charge can range from 10-80%. It is worth it to shop around. Be sure they are not exclusive, which means you can only offer your book there.

Try to adhere to a format that works on multiple readers. Amazon, for example, has the Kindle reader that works with the .mobi format (although it has been converted again after this point to create the file format native to the Kindle reader.) Amazon bought Mobipocket for just this purpose. You can find formatting details both at Amazon and at Mobipocket. PDFs have an advantage in that you can preserve the formatting you've created and thereby maintain a bit more of the "book" appearance despite the reading platform. There are dozens of eBook readers on market as of this writing and by the time you read this, they may number more. Take a bit of time to research the prevalent formats, also .epub is always a safe bet. It is the agreed upon eBook standard and will either be directly read, or be easily converted into what the desired reader needs. It will not afford you as much creative input with regard to formatting that the .pdf allows, but creates a very small file in terms of storage and downloading time needed.

A word here on text editors. Since text-editing software is immensely popular, indeed, you may have written your book in it, it would seem that it could be used to create the eBook. While it is allowed in some of the conversion programs, the software tends to add in a great deal of information that is pertinent to the software and not to the document being created. Thus, you can end up with "garbage code" which will not help your formatting translation and it will increase the file size. If you are converting books professionally, read information regarding the .epub format. In addition, look for reading material on how you can use a simple text editing software to prepare your book. There are alternatives to using different text editors.

eBook distributors. While many of the eBook bookstores also act as a distributor, they will not have the range of devices or file types you need. Thus, it often makes sense to go through an eBook distributor who works with many eBook sellers. Their role is to provide the conversion into the standard formats for you and then register your book through all the avenues open to that format. Think of it as hub to all the eBook selling outlets available. These are often also very helpful sites to visit as they provide a great deal of information about formatting, techniques for marketing, content creation and the options available in each of the eBook readers. They will keep a small part of each sale for their part in the process.

Audio Books

Audio books have transformed over the last decade as well. It used to be that books were recorded by audio professionals and then edited with sophisticated equipment before being duplicated on cassette tapes and packaged for consumers. This could be a difficult undertaking, evidenced by the number of books, which were never offered in this format.

Audio books, of course, are extremely convenient when you drive, exercise or work around the house. They keep your hands free while you still are enjoying the book's contents. The sets were very expensive, often costing more than $50 for just a single book, which made them ideal for libraries who could lend them out, but less ideal for individuals who would listen once and then donate or try to re-sell them. It was a cumbersome concept. They were very expensive to produce, as a professional studio must be outfitted and a voice-over professional engaged who would spend the necessary hours in the studio recording. There were also editing and mixing professionals, followed by the company who duplicated the tapes and packaged them.

This has all changed and now you can actually make your own audio book if you like.

Preparing for Your Audio Book

You will first need to make sure your manuscript is suitable for reading. If you are planning to do your own recording, you will naturally feel very at home with the wording and the cadence. Be sure to read the book aloud first as you may be surprised to find awkward phrasings you thought were otherwise fine. If someone else will be doing the reading, be sure a readable copy is available and comfortable for him or her to read. They may even have a list of specifications with regard to font, size, leading, line length and reading script page size they will want you to follow.

You no longer need an entire recording studio to get a decent sound recorded. For some people, using a simple headset with microphone works very well. Test out the equipment you may already have. If that doesn't work well for you, visit a music store or computer supercenter where you can try out some other options. The office supply store may also be a good source as they have setups for people who will be doing transcriptions, answering telephones and doing voice commanded software in the business arena.

Both PCs and Macs have recording software built into their operating systems. They are simple and don't necessarily let you record long segments, but their attraction is that they won't cost you additional money. Depending on your book, this may or may not work for you. There is inexpensive recording software available on both platforms; do an internet search and use some trials until you find one that works well for you.

If your pocket is a bit deeper, you may opt for one of the professional recording packages. These will allow you to record lengths that are dictated by the amount of storage you have available. Note here: audio files are very large and you will want to have plenty of disk space before you get started.

The more sophisticated packages also give you the opportunity to edit, combine tracks, and add sound effects or musical backgrounds. In addition, you can filter the sounds to eliminate popping, cracking, electronic hums, etc. You can also do transitions and accurately edit to specific desired time lengths.

If you are using a voice over professional, chances are they will be able to do all this for you and your result will be a fully edited, professional product. You can find such people on the Internet and they are available on a freelance basis. Search some of the freelancing websites and post a project along with a request for a brief voice sample and it becomes an easy prospect to choose an artist. Most have a studio already set up in their home or place of business.

Once you have your recordings you can look for a CD manufacturer with duplication services. There are many available and you'll find them through the Internet. Some even offer disk-at-a-time fulfillment with direct shipping. These companies can also do editing for you and will offer design services for your CD imprinting and the packaging. Choose packaging that will mail safely or you'll have customer service issues to deal with.

Keep branding in mind as you package the audio version of your book. It's a good idea to coordinate it with your paper book. While people will understand that production costs in audio books will require somewhat higher prices, try to stay within the range of your competition.

Many booksellers will carry your audio book. They will also have programs set up to handle author/distributors. However, they will ask for a hefty portion of the sales. Be sure to do the numbers and make ensure you're ending up with a profit. They will also ask to return unsold copies so keep your packaging/production costs to a minimum.

One of the new trends in audio is to sell your book audio through your own website as a serialized download. This can be accomplished using streaming technology or as a direct download, depending on the size of the book files. If you are going to offer a streaming experience, be sure your hosting company can accommodate the bandwidth. A popular book could get a flood of listeners and the added, sudden traffic could shut down your server. Exceeding the bandwidth allowance from your hosting package could also result in your having monster overcharges, so be sure you understand what your package entitles you to compared to what you expect to host.

There are audio booksellers available through the Internet. These companies are set up to handle either streaming or downloadable work and while they will collect a sizeable portion of the profit; it's just a file and costs you nothing to let them sell as many copies as they can. They also come with the benefit of having an existing customer base and marketing program, so you're just along for the hayride.

The Podcasting Generation

If you use the Internet, you are probably aware of podcasting and may have listened to a few. Think of podcasting as having a radio show on the Internet. There are a few sources that provide free podcasts services. These podcasts are produced by major television and film studios.

You would create a podcast the same way you do an audio book except that your presentation would be more for informational or marketing purposes. You can use podcasts to distribute your audio book, but most are offered free of charge so this probably wouldn't fit your needs.

Many podcasts are recorded by former radio disc jockeys who seek to establish their own listening networks. A very popular example would be major recording facilities who offer to host dozens of weekly shows, which are broadcast in video or just audio formats across the Internet and through many popular radio stations. A few well-known jockeys income is said to be well over a million dollars each year from this enterprise and it doesn't take a professional television or radio background to start this. Some shows are free and the income is derived from advertising revenue.

In Summary

The important thing to realize is that you aren't confined to paper, and aren't confined to one presentation of your book any longer. You can re-purpose your content in many different and additionally interesting ways. Each of these beckons to yet another audience and the networking possibilities are endless. Don't be afraid to create this yourself, it just takes a bit of research to create a commendable product.

Your Business in a Book Journal

For the next 30 days, think and write about your successes and challenges to becoming an author. At the conclusion of the thirty-day cycle, please send a testimonial of your progress, if this book has been helpful to you. We would love to hear from you. Email testimonials to:

valerie@the90dayauthor.com

Day 1

Day 2

Day 3

Day 4

Day 5

Day 6

Day 7

Day 8

Day 9

Day 10

Day 11

Day 12

Day 13

Day 14

Day 15

Day 16

Day 17

Day 18

Day 19

Day 20

Day 21

Day 22

Day 23

Day 24

Day 25

Day 26

Day 27

Day 28

Day 29

Day 30

Motivational Quotes

Do not abandon wisdom, and she will protect you; love her, and she will keep you safe. Getting wisdom is the most important thing you can do. Whatever else you get, get insight. Love wisdom, and she will make you great. Embrace her, and she will bring you honor."

Prov. 4:6-8

WISDOM WILL ADD YEARS TO YOUR LIFE.

Prov. 9:11

LISTEN TO WHAT IS WISE AND TRY TO UNDERSTAND IT. YES, BEG FOR KNOWLEDGE; PLEAD FOR INSIGHT.

Prov 2:2-3

AN IDEA WELL-EXPRESSED IS LIKE A
DESIGN OF GOLD, SET IN SILVER.

Prov 25:11

ALWAYS REMEMBER WHAT YOU HAVE LEARNED. YOUR EDUCATION IS YOUR LIFE—GUARD IT WELL.

Prov 4:13

BE CAREFUL HOW YOU THINK; YOUR LIFE
IS SHAPED BY YOUR THOUGHTS.

Prov. 4:23

PLAN CAREFULLY WHAT YOU DO, AND
WHATEVER YOU DO WILL TURN OUT
RIGHT.

Prov. 4:26

BE GENEROUS, AND YOU WILL BE PROSPEROUS. HELP OTHERS, AND YOU WILL BE HELPED.

Prov. 11:25

DO YOURSELF A FAVOR AND LEARN ALL
YOU CAN; THEN REMEMBER WHAT YOU
LEARN AND YOU WILL PROSPER.

Prov. 19:8

PAY ATTENTION TO YOUR TEACHER AND
LEARN ALL YOU CAN.

Prov. 23:11

THE WISE IN HEART ARE CALLED
PRUDENT, UNDERSTANDING, AND
KNOWING, AND WINSOME SPEECH
INCREASES LEARNING [IN BOTH SPEAKER
AND LISTENER.

Prov. 16:21

A SOUND, HEALTHY BODY AND A
CHEERFUL ATTITUDE ARE MORE
VALUABLE THAN GOLD AND JEWELS.

Sirach 30:15

WISDOM CAN MAKE YOUR LIFE PLEASANT
AND LEAD YOU SAFELY THROUGH IT.

Prov. 3:17

IF THE AX IS DULL AND ITS EDGE UNSHARPENED, MORE STRENGTH IS NEEDED, BUT SKILL WILL BRING SUCCESS.

Eccl. 10:10 (NIV)

SO I REALIZED THAT ALL WE CAN DO IS BE
HAPPY AND DO THE BEST WE CAN WHILE
WE ARE STILL ALIVE.

Eccl. 3:12

I ALONE KNOW THE PLANS I HAVE FOR
YOU, PLANS TO BRING YOU PROSPERITY
AND NOT DISASTER, PLANS TO BRING
ABOUT THE FUTURE YOU HOPE FOR.

Jer 29:11

About the Author

Valerie Sherrod is an entrepreneur, author, book publishing strategist, graphic designer, and humanitarian. She is also considered a multi-gifted artist who is also known for her wisdom, wit and sense of humor.

The author is also founder of Sherrod Publishing and Enterprises, which focuses on the different aspects of her publishing empire, including the 90 Day Author, the 90 Day Author Kids, Couleure Fashion Magazine and Dominion 12 Comics.

Valerie has worked with many authors to get their works in print by navigating the challenging, yet rewarding process.

Passionate about what she does, the central theme of her message is to help business owners become forerunners in his/her field of expertise in 90 days or less.

With over 12 years of experience in the book publishing industry, the 90 Day Author was created to serve a specific group of business owners whose desire is to set themselves apart from average business owners by becoming authors.

In her community, she has taught life skills to women and teenagers, engaged in foreign missions, and has aided in the development of leaders and aspiring business owners by providing consultation.

Visit The 90 Day Author at **www.the90dayauthor.com** to become the next forerunner in your field of expertise.

IT ALL STARTS WITH JUST *ONE* BOOK!

www.ingramcontent.com/pod-product-compliance
Lightning Source LLC
Chambersburg PA
CBHW072206090426
42740CB00012B/2410